IF FC

MW01286984

Greater Than a Tourist Book Series
Reviews from Readers

I think the series is wonderful and beneficial for tourists to get information before visiting the city.

-Seckin Zumbul, Izmir Turkey

I am a world traveler who has read many trip guides but this one really made a difference for me. I would call it a heartfelt creation of a local guide expert instead of just a guide.

-Susy, Isla Holbox, Mexico

New to the area like me, this is a must have!

 -Joe, Bloomington, USA

This is a good series that gets down to it when looking for things to do at your destination without having to read a novel for just a few ideas.

-Rachel, Monterey, USA

i

Good information to have to plan my trip to this destination.

-Pennie Farrell, Mexico

Great ideas for a port day.

-Mary Martin USA

Aptly titled, you won't just be a tourist after reading this book. You'll be greater than a tourist!

-Alan Warner, Grand Rapids, USA

Even though I only have three days to spend in San Miguel in an upcoming visit, I will use the author's suggestions to guide some of my time there. An easy read - with chapters named to guide me in directions I want to go.

-Robert Catapano, USA

Great insights from a local perspective! Useful information and a very good value!

-Sarah, USA

This series provides an in-depth experience through the eyes of a local. Reading these series will help you to travel the city in with confidence and it'll make your journey a unique one.

-Andrew Teoh, Ipoh, Malaysia

GREATER THAN A TOURIST- MISSISSIPPI USA

50 Travel Tips from a Local

Ellycia Villescas

Cover designed by: Ivana Stamenkovic
Cover Image: https://pixabay.com/en/minnesota-mississippi-skyline-422264/

CZYK Publishing Since 2011.

Greater Than a Tourist
Visit our website at www.GreaterThanaTourist.com

Lock Haven, PA
All rights reserved.
ISBN: 9781724105882

>TOURIST

50 TRAVEL TIPS FROM A LOCAL

BOOK DESCRIPTION

Are you excited about planning your next trip?

Do you want to try something new?

Would you like some guidance from a local?

If you answered yes to any of these questions, then this Greater Than a Tourist book is for you.

Greater Than a Tourist- Mississippi, USA, by Ellycia Villescas, offers the inside scoop on traveling through the state. Most travel books tell you how to travel like a tourist. Although there is nothing wrong with that, as part of the Greater Than a Tourist series, this book will give you travel tips from someone who has lived at your next travel destination.

In these pages, you will discover advice that will help you throughout your stay. This book will not tell you exact addresses or store hours but instead will give you excitement and knowledge from a local that you may not find in other smaller print travel books.

Travel like a local. Slow down, stay in one place, and get to know the people and the culture. By the time you finish this book, you will be eager and prepared to travel to your next destination.

TABLE OF CONTENTS

DEDICATION

This book is dedicated to Charlie, Gretchen, Nicole, Robert, and Teresa. Without you, I would not have been able to grow into the woman I am today. Thanks to you, I am someone who desires to travel and always seek out new opportunities, regardless of how uncomfortable the unknown is.

The many stories, road trips, National Parks, new cities, and relocations have all rendered an adventurous spirit in me. It is with great love and gratitude that I thank you for shaping that part of me and the many others pieces as well. With your support and encouragement, I have become the person I am today. My adventures will never stop, in part to your influence, don't worry…I am currently planning my next adventure…

ABOUT THE AUTHOR

Over 17 years, nine moves and seven different states, today I find myself living in the Magnolia State. Born into a family with a sense of adventure, it's only fitting that as I have grown that I too have begun seeking my own experiences and adventures. Until the age of 22, I had moved with my family up until my college years. Shortly after graduation, I took the plunge, without them, and moved 600 miles away.

In 2015, along with Chris and our fur-child, our little family went off on our own to begin our life in 'The 'Sip.' Our time here in Mississippi has been far greater than I could have ever imagined. Regardless of where you travel, whether you enjoy the place or hate it, remember that you can always find at least one single piece to love about anywhere you go. Keep that in mind during along your journey in life and you'll always find adventure.

HOW TO USE THIS BOOK

The Greater Than a Tourist book series was written by someone who has lived in an area for over three months. The goal of this book is to help travelers either dream or experience different locations by providing opinions from a local. The author has made suggestions based on their own experiences. Please do your own research before traveling to the area in case the suggested places are unavailable.

FROM THE PUBLISHER

Traveling can be one of the most important parts of a person's life. The anticipation and memories that you have are some of the best. As a publisher of the Greater Than a Tourist book series, as well as the popular 50 Things to Know book series, we strive to help you learn about new places, spark your imagination, and inspire you. Wherever you are and whatever you do I wish you safe, fun, and inspiring travel.

Lisa Rusczyk Ed. D.
CZYK Publishing

OUR STORY

Traveling is a passion of the "Greater than a Tourist" series creator. Lisa studied abroad in college, and for their honeymoon Lisa and her husband toured Europe. During her travels to Malta, an older man tried to give her some advice based on his own experience living on the island since he was a young boy. She was not sure if she should talk to the stranger but was interested in his advice. When traveling to some places she was wary to talk to locals because she was afraid that they weren't being genuine. Through her travels, Lisa learned how much locals had to share with tourists. Lisa created the "Greater Than a Tourist" book series to help connect people with locals. A topic that locals are very passionate about sharing.

WELCOME TO
> TOURIST

INTRODUCTION

"Traveling – it leaves you speechless, then it turns you into a storyteller."

– Ibn Battuta

Over the course of our time in Mississippi, we have had many experiences within the state. The goal of this book is to offer the reader a little bit of history, tidbits of advice and a long list of places to visit while traveling in the great state of Mississippi.

1. M-I-SS-I-SS-I-PP-I

For the record, it is *still* okay to spell out the state the same way you did when you first learned to spell and in US Geography. On occasion, the locals still need to.

Why visit Mississippi? Why not?! The Magnolia State sprawls across six different regions, each unique and different from the rest. In culture, heritage, scenery, one region is not a mirror image of another. Your experiences will vary where you travel to, but will also offer an abundance of different experiences you have throughout the state.

Consider this book as your official tour guide, highlighting the best features in the state regardless of the region you will be visiting. In addition to the personal suggestions, you will find additional links to help you out when planning for your travels through the Magnolia State. Whether you are looking for a history lesson, beaches, The Blues, or some local cuisine, 'The 'Sip' has it all.

2. WHEN TO VISIT

If there is one thing Mississippi is universally known for, it is probably the humidity. Regardless of the time of year you are planning to visit, humidity is present nearly 350 of the 365 days a year. Prior to visiting, it will be important to make plans for the activities you will want to do. With a multitude of different options, indoor/outdoor, wet/dry, or possibly seasonal, looking up the local weather beforehand is vital when making your plans to visit.

Typically the climate is warm year-round, the best times to visit for non-seasonal activities would be in the month of March, or October- November. During these periods, typically the weather is in the 70s °F, with a slight to moderate chance of rain. The humidity is also typically lower during this period as well. During these months of the year, it is likely that hotel rates should be lower than during peak months of travel; the summer months and holiday season.

3. Y'ALL IS A PROPER NOUN

Perhaps one of the most distinct signs that you are in the South is the common use of the word "y'all." A word of advice to travelers, adopt the saying, it is part of one's perfect grammar in Mississippi.

Similar to the phrases "youse," and "yinz," "y'all" is the simplified way to address a group of people down in the South. As every region in the United States has the dialects that differentiate them from other parts of the country, y'all is just one of the many that make the South, and Mississippians unique.

Feel free to begin testing the waters and using this phrase during your travels, a simple "how are y'all today" will help you fit right in, versus a "how are you."

4. A MISSISSIPPI BUCKET LIST

When thinking of Mississippi, what comes to mind? The Bible Belt, country-cookin', the Deep South, the Cotton Gin? While many of those are associated with the state, there are many more reasons to visit:

- Mississippi's Hot Tamale Trail
- Mississippi Blues Trail
- (Legal) Sports Betting

Covering 48,000 square miles, Mississippi's landscape is vast and different from one part of the state to the next. The state can be covered from North to South in about five hours, in two and a half hours from East to West.

Prior to planning a trip, it is important to know what part of the state you are going to and what you are looking for during your travels.

5. WHERE Y'ALL GOING?

As large as the state is as are the different regions that sprawl across Mississippi:

- The Hills
- The Mississippi Delta
- The Golden Triangle
- Central Mississippi
- The Pine Belt
- The Gulf Coast

Each region is unique to itself, as are the experiences that are available within them. Due to each region's uniqueness, the activities within these regions will vary from one to another. These tips will help identify what makes each region special and to help you plan your trip based on what you want.

"The Mississippi towns are comely, clean, well build, and pleasing to the eye, and cheering to the spirit."

– Mark Twain

6. THE HILLS

The Hills, situated North Mississippi, are given this name for the hills that roll across the landscape as your drive by. While traveling through this area you will travel over marshes and pass many small lakes. This part of the state is absolutely beautiful, and weather can typically be cooler than the south-central and southern half of the state.

7. THE HILLS– CITIES TO VISIT

This area of Mississippi boasts some metropolitan areas worth visiting:

- This area of Mississippi boasts some metropolitan areas worth visiting:
- Grenada- In the "City that Smiles," this is one of the best places in the state to cast a fishing line out and spend the day on, or near, the water.

- Holly Springs- Founded in 1836 and boasting 90 Antebellum Era homes, you will feel like you're taking a trip back in time.
- Oxford- Home to the University of Mississippi, a campus that is bound to be packed by tailgaters on any Fall Saturday.
- Southaven- Directly across from the state border of Tennessee, with a mere 15-minute drive you can make your way to the world-famous Beale Street in Memphis.

"Only remember west of the Mississippi it's a little more look, see, act. A little less rationalize, comment talk." – F. Scott Fitzgerald

8. THE HILLS- GRENADA, MS

Nestled right next to Grenada Lake, Grenada was once home to the Choctaw Indian Tribe. Founded by European Americans in 1836, the town was once known for its production of cotton.

Many of the popular activities are outdoors, including: the Chakchiuma Swamp, Haserway Wetland

Nature Trail, and the Tallahatchie National Wildlife Refuge. While those activities are available year-round, the most popular event every year is "Thunder on Water," which is held in June of each year. This event promotes safe boating with a carnival, fireworks, music, and car shows!

"Books were my pass to personal freedom. I learned to read at the age of three, and soon discovered that there was a whole world to conquer that went beyond our farm in Mississippi." – Oprah Winfrey

9. THE HILLS- HOLLY SPRINGS, MS

Take a trip back in time and visit Holly Springs, "Mississippi's best-kept secret." The city dates back to pre-Civil War time and continues to boast hospitality you will only find in the South. There are many activities to do while visiting this gorgeous town!

Tie up your hiking boots and go for a walk on the six trails within the Holly Springs National Forrest. If you're not in exercising, schedule a tour to visit the Marshall County Historical Museum or the Magnolia

Mansion. To make sure you don't go hungry, don't forget to grab a bite to eat at the famous Phillips Grocery…you won't regret it!

"The attorney general would call at 5 o'clock in the evening and say: 'Tomorrow morning we are going to try to integrate the University of Mississippi. Get us a memo on what we're likely to do, and what we can do if the governor sends the National Guard there." – Harold H. Green

10. THE HILLS- OXFORD, MS

On a Saturday in the South, you most certainly need to add a visit to "The Grove" to your agenda! The Grove is surrounded by Oak, Elm, and Magnolia Trees and located on the University of Mississippi's campus. It holds a tradition of being dressed in your Sunday's Best and being the prime location for tailgating before an Ole Miss Football game.

No one to tailgate with? Not a problem! Ole Miss hosts one of the friendliest campuses in the South Eastern Conference (aka The SEC). Stroll up to a tailgate and mention that you are visiting, you'll be welcomed with open arms! Don't let the chandeliers or house-sized tents intimidate you, every Southerner loves to hosts guests! Oh, and be sure to add "Hotty Toddy" to your memory during your visit to this city.

Represented as 'a small town with big style,' Downtown Oxford will not disappoint. Sprawled along the streets in downtown you will find local boutiques, the oldest department store in the South, a national renowned bookstore, and restaurants that will make you drool with just a whiff of the food. For the foodies of the world, below are the must-visit places sorted by meal:

- Coffee/ Pastries- Bottletree Bakery

Serving up breakfast and lunch, the café is located in downtown offering a great spot to relax or get in some good people watching. It is popular to local residents and college students in the town.

- Lunch- Bouré

Overlooking the town square from the second-floor veranda, it offers beautiful views in addition to great food. Serving up lunch and dinner you'll be sure to find some "down-home cooking" mixed with an edge.

- Dinner- McEwen's

Offering an opportunity to escape to an intimate setting, paired with a backdrop of hardwood floors and exposed brick. The food is just as beautiful as the aesthetic of the appearance. You can also feel great about eating here as it is a member of the Project Green Fork, an initiative which is helping restaurants in the South lessen their impact on the environment.

- Brunch- The Oxford Grillehouse

Bottomless mimosas and Bloody Marys, a build your own mimosa/ Bloody Mary bar?! If this alone is drawing you in, head on down to The Oxford Grillehouse, located in the town square, the food is as eye-catching as it is filling going down.

"I am fascinated by the places that music comes from, like fife-and-drum blues from southern Mississippi or Cajun music out of Lafayette, Louisiana, I love that stuff. It's like the beginning of rock and roll: something comes down from the hills, and something comes up from the Delta."

– Robbie Roberston

11. THE HILLS- SOUTHAVEN, MS

If you are staying in Southaven, Graceland is a must visit when you're this close! The former home of The King of Rock n' Roll, Elvis Presley. The National Historic Landmark is nearly 14 acres, over 17,500 square feet, and the second most visited home in the United States (behind the White House).

The mansion offers tours and up-close viewings of the heartfelt belongings that once belonged to the Legend. It's a must visit if you're a fan of Rock n' Roll.

"My parents were working in a hospital in Memphis. But I didn't live there for any length of time that I remember. The first thing I remember is the town in Mississippi that I live in now, Charleston."

– Morgan Freeman

12. THE MISSISSIPPI DELTA

The Delta, located in the Northwestern part of the state and is bound between the Mississippi and Yazoo Rivers. The area includes an abundance of farmland, is rich in Native American history, and is most commonly known as the birthplace of the Blues.

13. THE DELTA- CITIES TO VISIT

The Delta Region has cities that are known worldwide thanks to the Blues:

- Belzoni, MS- In addition to being known as the Farm-Raised Catfish Capital of the World, this city also boasts its importance to the Civil Rights movement.
- Clarksdale, MS- This is one of the friendliest towns you will ever visit, no matter where you are going you will be greeted with a smile. When visiting, make sure you reciprocate that friendliness with a smile, or

even a "hello" and you won't leave as a stranger in this town.

- Greenville, MS- Sitting on the Mississippi River, Greenville is home to one of the three only bridges over the mighty Mississippi River. Connected to the state of Mississippi are the states of Arkansas and Louisiana.

- Greenwood, MS- Upon entering the city limits, you will instantly feel the small town vibe that Greenwood gives off. Once known as the "Cotton Capital of the World," today it is known as the "Gateway to the Mississippi Delta."

"I would sit on the street corners in my hometown and I would play. People would always compliment me on Gospel tunes, but they would tip me when I played the Blues."

– B. B. King

14. THE DELTA-BELZONI, MS

While Belzoni is a small town, it is a small town that has historical importance with the role that its citizens played during the Civil Rights Movement. While markers are located throughout the state, the Mississippi Freedom Trail has a marker honoring Reverend George Lee and detailing his contribution to the Civil Rights Movement in Mississippi.

Also included in the history of Belzoni, the city has been known as the Catfish Capital of the World since 1976. With over 117 catfish farms in the county, more than 75% of all catfish consumed in the United States every year comes from the state of Mississippi.

Open Monday through Friday, the Catfish Museum is a great place to learn about the farm-raised catfish industry. Walking through the museum, you will get an idea of day-to-day activities for farmers and you can even pick up a few recipes along the way. Once a year, The World Catfish Festival is held every spring. The event includes local vendors, live music and a catfish eating contest.

"The Mississippi Delta is the fastest-disappearing land on the planet."

– Nina Easton

15. THE DELTA- CLARKSDALE, MS

If you are traveling in the Mississippi Delta, Clarksdale is a city that you must visit. Statewide, Clarksdale is known for three things in particular: museums, good food, and live music.

How has Rock 'n Roll and Soul music influenced the culture of music as it is today? Visit the Rock & Roll Blues Museum to find out. Packed with memorabilia ranging from the 1920's through the 1970's, you can take a tour and walk through the evolution of America's music. These styles transformed music into what we know today, all around the globe.

When looking for a bite to eat, look no farther than the Ground Zero Blues Club. Featured on The Food Network and The Travel Channel, there is no question that this is your one-stop shop for some grub and entertainment. For lunch or dinner, you will leave with a full belly. The menu includes 'southern fixin's,' my personal favorite, the Catfish BLT. Once voted onto the list of "Top 100 Bars and Nightclubs in America," Wednesday through Saturday evenings, live music is performed every night.

"I've always been in love with that Delta-flavored music...the music that came from Mississippi and Memphis and, especially New Orleans. When I was 14, I was in a wanna-be New Orleans band in Toronto."

– Robbie Robertson

16. THE DELTA- GREENVILLE, MS

Once home to a prehistoric Native American civilization, evidence of their community is still visible to this day. The Winterville Mounds are a historical site where visitors can get a hands-on experience of where, and how, this group lived. Upon entering the site, you will see what seems to resemble a smaller version of the Great Pyramids in Egypt.

Today there are 12 mounds, created by the digging, transporting and shaping of dirt by hand, that visitors can view while traveling along the walking trails on the site. In modern U.S. history, the other known excavated prehistoric mound site is located outside of Saint Louis, Missouri. Visiting the Winterville Mounds is truly a unique opportunity that is hard to experience anywhere else in the United States.

The Tamale Trail is also what Greenville is famously known for. The trail has over ten different restaurants, featured on the Trail, that are located in Greenville. Greenville is a hub for many tasting stops along the Tamale Trail. For additional specifics on the on the Tamale Trail in Mississippi, stop in for yourself at a tamale joint in Greenville and visit tip #43 to make your taste buds water and read up on the history of the Trail. Make sure to add Doe's Eat Place onto your list when visiting the Greenville as well. The family tamale recipe dates back to 1903 and is just as delicious as the day it was created.

"I've always been fascinated by the Mississippi River and the way of life in these small river towns."

– Daniel Woodrell

17. THE DELTA- GREENWOOD, MS

The Mississippi Delta is a region that is rich in its cultural heritage. With a diverse history and open-arm hospitality, Greenwood is no exception. During your visit, you will be able to slow down and relax with the good music, great company, and delicious food.

One way to spend your trip would be to visit the Back in the Day Museum. You will be able to get a tour and hands-on experience exploring the history of the Blues, Baptist Town and African-American culture in the Delta. Tours are given by natives of Greenwood. Open Monday through Saturday, be sure to call ahead to schedule a visit.

If you have ever seen *The Help*, a film by DreamWorks Pictures, much of the movie itself was filmed in Greenwood, Mississippi. Representing

Jackson, Mississippi in the 1960's, the movie (and novel) gives you a front-row seat and takes you back in time. With the endless cotton fields and magnolia trees, Greenwood was hand-picked by producers for the location of the film.

Many of the homes that the characters lived in can also be visited, although they are private property, you can still view them. You can also visit where the location of the Baptist Church, the hotel, and bookstore from the film are in town. You can truly feel as if you are walking in the 1960s visiting some of these locations, it's almost as if they were frozen in time.

After a busy day of activity, head on down to The Crystal Grill. Featured on The Food Network, the grill has been open for more than 75 years. Local favorites on the menu include the hot tamales, fried catfish and homemade pies. Greenwood locals will go on record saying that these are some of the best entrees in the Delta Region.

*"Growing up on the plantation
there in Mississippi, I would work
Monday through Saturday noon. I'd
go to town on Saturday afternoons,
sit on the street corner, and I'd sing
and play."*

– B. B. King

18. THE GOLDEN TRIANGLE

Connecting the three cities of Columbus, Starkville, and West Point, the Golden Triangle is located in the Eastern Region of the state and spreads over 60 miles.

19. THE TRIANGLE- CITIES TO VISIT

When visiting this region of the state, the most popular cities to visit are the ones that give The Golden Triangle its name:

- Columbus- Prior to its founding in 1821, Columbus was referred to as Possum Town, a name given by the Choctaw Indians who lived in the area.
- Starkville- Recognized as the most populated city in The Golden Triangle, Starkville is dotted by boutiques and the mom and pop restaurants that line the city streets.
- Tupelo- Memphis is most commonly associated with Elvis since it is the home of Graceland What many visitors don't know is that Tupelo is the where the King was born and lived until his early teenage years.
- West Point- Commonly known as a retirement community for those wanting to live out their 'Golden Years,' you can visit one of the best golf courses in the state or

visit hundred-year-old plantation homes in this city.

"If you write a book about a bygone period that lies east of Mississippi, then it's a historical novel. If it's west of the Mississippi, it's a western."

– Louis L'Amour

20. THE TRIANGLE-COLUMBUS, MS

Represented as "The city that has it all," Columbus truly offers any possible activity that you could want to do. Visit historic homes, learn about America's greatest playwright, or spend time in the outdoors. You will definitely find an activity to keep you busy during your stay in this city.

Columbus boasts a kind of history and heritage that it is proud of. You can schedule a tour to visit historic homes that are one-of-a-kind to the region. You can also go on an African American historical tour and learn about the influences (Catfish Alley anyone?), that have contributed to creating the city that is Columbus.

Located on the Tennessee-Tombigbee Waterway, Columbus also offers many recreational activities. Among the many parks sprawled across the city, time can be spent at the Splash Pads, Skateboard Park, and Bark Park. Columbus also has four different top-notch golf courses for those looking for a relaxing day outdoors.

For adrenaline seekers, plan a visit to one of the two speedways located in the city: The Columbus Speedway and The Magnolia Motor Speedway. Both vary in seasonal activities and events, so be sure to call and ask for information when planning your visit.

"When I chose Mississippi State, of course, I dreamed about being a big-time college football player. But I'm so grateful that actually became a reality- and it became a reality in a small town."

– Dak Prescott

21. THE TRIANGLE-STARKVILLE, MS

The main attraction for visitors to Starkville is that the city is home to Mississippi State University, another school located in the SEC. Being the home to a state university, the city definitely gives off a college town vibe. Many visitors coming into town are visiting to attend a football game, or other university-sponsored sporting events. A word of advice, don't forget to bring your cowbell on your next visit to a football game in Starkville. It's a necessity for a visit to Davis Wade Stadium.

While being dubbed a "college town," the city also boasts many locally owned boutique and restaurants. Popular shopping areas include the streets in Downtown Starkville. Here you can stock up for game day apparel, a new pair of kicks, or just window shop. When looking for restaurants, there are so many in this city that they need to be organized by meal:

- Coffee/ Pastries- 929 Coffee Bar Located in Downtown Starkville, you can come here knowing your pastries will be baked fresh daily and coffee will be of the best quality. Open from 7 AM to 9 PM, count on this to be your go-to place when needing a good "cup of joe," or a sweet to cure your sugar tooth.

- Lunch- Bulldog Burger Company
  With a promise to serve "big, juicy, handmade" burgers look no further than the Bulldog Burger Company. When visiting this Mississippi restaurant, you can rest assured knowing that you will be served the best burger in town.
- Dinner- The Veranda
  Located near Mississippi State University, The Veranda offers a variety of fresh seafood on their menu. Mouthwatering entrees such as Mahi Mahi, filet mignon, ribeye and pork tenderloin are regularly available. Be sure to ask what the daily specials are, you won't want to miss out!
- Brunch- Restaurant Tyler
  Restaurant Tyler is a prime hot-spot to get brunch on Sunday mornings. Their menu includes a mixture of traditional brunch items (i.e. French toast), southern

brunch items (i.e. Chicken and Waffles), and Blue Plates (tip #46) available on their menu. Unless you have a party of seven or more, reservations are not accepted so be sure to visit early or plan to wait. No worries though, they make a great Bloody Mary and mimosa!

- Happy Hour- The Guest Room Located in a prime location on Main Street, The Guest Room offers one of the best happy hours in the city. Offering classic drinks like the Sazerac, a tradition of New Orleans, and the Old Fashion, the prices can't be beaten! If hungry, you may want to grab a snack here. Also featured on the happy hour menu are sliders, dips and cheese plates. Open Tuesday through Friday, happy hour is 4:30PM-6PM, be sure to stop by.

If your visit to Starkville is planned during the fall and happens to be on a Saturday where Mississippi State Football is playing a home game, you're in luck! The New South Weekends are hosted after every home football game. Featuring downtown shops and restaurants, the New South Weekends offer specials following the game! Be sure to look online to see which restaurants are participating during the weekly rotation.

"In the '50s, listening to Elvis and others on the radio in Bombay- it didn't feel alien. Noises made by a truck driver from Tupelo, Mississippi, seemed relevant to a middle-class kid growing up on the other side of the world. That has always fascinated me."

– Salman Rushdie

22. THE TRIANGLE- TUPELO, MS

Sitting in the Americana Music Triangle, Tupelo is connected to other great cities known for their music; Memphis and Nashville, Tennessee. When visiting Tupelo, the birthplace of "The King," there are many activities that separate this city from other musical hotspots. Plan a visit to the Elvis Presley

Birthplace and Museum, visit the Elvis Presley homecoming statue, and stop into the Tupelo Hardware Company (where he made his decision to pick up his first guitar).

Be sure to take a stroll through Downtown Tupelo during your visit. Streets are lined with locally owned businesses, a few that you definitely need to check out:

- Shockley's- Grab a cup of coffee, order some breakfast or lunch, and you won't be disappointed when you visit this mom-and-pop restaurant.

- Reed's Department Store- Reed's has been in business for over 125 years, offering a wide selection of colorful clothing, you can surely pick out an outfit made for a Southerner: complete with a bow tie, or a sundress.

- Neon Pig Café- Featured on The Food Network show "Super Southern Eats," the décor, ambiance, and food are no joke. You'll leave with a full belly, and still a full wallet.

- Blue Canoe- Also a top rated restaurant in Tupelo, it is a "laid back, funky joint known as Tupelo's home for original live music."

After a day on the town, spend time outdoors and head to the Tupelo Buffalo Park. Originally a cattle ranch in 1997, buffalos were introduced to the ranch over time. At one point the herd grew to over 300! Since the early 2000s, the land has grown and other animals have been introduced including: lions, lemurs, camels, and more. A great adventure for a family, couples, or solo travelers, ask about the VIP tour to get an opportunity to get up close to the animals!

"Mark Twain gave us an insight into the life on the Mississippi at the turn of the century."

– Bob Newhart

23. THE TRIANGLE– WEST POINT, MS

The city of West Point is currently in a revival period for its industries and the Main Street in town. West Point is transforming its community through a rebirth of its neighborhoods and downtown area. In addition to the many parks, historic buildings and downtown streets that are lined with businesses, West Point also offers a variety of recreational activities available year round.

A fulfilling way to spend your day will include a visit to the Waverley Mansion. Still standing, a plantation home from the Antebellum Era has now been converted into a historic house museum. In 1973 it was declared a National Historic Landmark. At Waverly, you will feel as if you were transported back in time to the 1840s during which it was constructed.

Featured as a stop on the Mississippi Blues Trail (see tip #45), be sure to plan some time to visit the Howlin' Wolf Blues Museum. The museum will walk you through the life and impact of Chester Arthur Burnett, aka "Howlin' Wolf." In the post-World War II era, 'Wolf' was a pioneer in reenergizing the Delta Blues.

Before your trip to West Point is over I would recommend visiting Anthony's Good Food Market. With daily specials, live music and events throughout the seasons you should definitely add it to your itinerary. The food is savory and the music is authentic.

"I rode on a float in one of the parades in Mississippi. It's an experience."

– Elliott Smith "

24. CENTRAL MISSISSIPPI

While traveling through this region you will notice that the landscape is fairly flat. You will see the transition from greenery, to farmland, to urbanicity in the region, which offers a variety of different activities when visiting the Central part of the state.

25. CENTRAL MS- CITIES TO VISIT

While hugging the I-20 corridor, these cities in Central Mississippi sprawl across the state connecting the Mighty Mississippi to the Alabama border:

- Jackson- Home to the state's Capital, originally founded in 1901, both the Senate and House of Representatives Chambers are located in the building.
- Meridian-During the 1850s the Mobile and Ohio Railroad and the Southern Railway both crossed through the city, this brought travelers to the area who founded the city in 1860.
- Ridgeland- Just on the outskirts of the Jackson city limits, Ridgeland offers a variety of activities for those searching for an outdoor adventure.
- Vicksburg- Seated on the bluffs of the Mississippi River, Vicksburg can attribute much of its history due to the role the city played during the Civil War.

"Growing up in Mississippi- a state that historically was a place of racial injustice, inequality and oppression- gave me the unique opportunity to experience first-hand the evolution of the Civil Rights Movement."

- Angela McGlowan

26. CENTRAL MS- JACKSON, MS

Welcome to Jackson, Mississippi, "The City of Soul." In addition to being the state's Capital, Jackson is also home to a budding art scene and is a city filled with diversity. When visiting this city, you can stop in and take a tour at one of the many museums; Mississippi History Museum, Civil Rights Museum, Sports Hall of Fame Museum, all of which are located near the city's center.

After a day of touring, I would recommend venturing to the Fondren neighborhood. Here you can grab a bite to eat while strolling among the many local shops featuring boutiques, art lofts, and local restaurants. Ending your night, I would recommend visiting Hal & Mal's Downtown. Operating as both a restaurant, bar and entertainment venue, it can almost be guaranteed that you can catch some live music any time during the week. Monday nights are "Blue Mondays," where you're bound to see some authentic Blues performers, often featuring young local artists.

> *"There's no real network, and every city in Mississippi is so spread out, so it isn't easy to drive around and pass out CDs. So when an artist from Natchez or Gold Coast or Meridian breaks out, they already know exactly what kind of an artist they want to be. The grind and hustle is so adamant."*

> – Big K.R.I.T.

27. CENTRAL MS- MERIDIAN, MS

Located 25 minutes away from the Mississippi-Alabama border, this charming city embraces its country music history and railroad heritage. Like many other Mississippi born musicians, Meridian has produced well-known artists including: Chris Ethridge (Country) and Jimmie Rodgers (Country/Blues), in addition to many more. In part to the musicians that began their careers in this city, Meridian has embraced the atmosphere of live music and frequently has live musical performances around town. This gives many visitors and locals the opportunity to experience local talent live and in person.

Labeled as one of Mississippi's "best-kept secrets" the Meridian Railroad Museum is located in the downtown historic district. Walking through this, *admission free*, museum visitors will see displays of model trains on mini railways. These active model trains can be seen traveling through, what looks like a picture perfect scene, of hills and country farms and then through the downtown area on the model. In remembrance of the first arrival of trains to Meridian in

1855, the museum pays tribute to the town's rich history with the railroads.

Before leaving Meridian, I would suggest visiting Weidmann's Restaurant. Dating back to 1870, Weidmann's has been creating and plating fresh and homemade southern cuisine. Located in Downtown Meridian, the location is central to many of the local businesses of the town.

"A lot of people I guess, well, some people change when they get in spotlights and everything, but you can take the girl out of Mississippi, but you can't take Mississippi out of the girl!"

– La'Porsha Renae

28. CENTRAL MS- RIDGELAND, MS

The city of Ridgeland embraces being outdoors with all activities. Leisure, exercising, shopping, dining, you can be sure you can partake in all of these activities outside. The Natchez Trace runs directly through the city and has miles of multi-use paths and trails that you can walk, run, or bike on. My personal favorite is visiting trails on the Trace early in the morning when it's still cool outside. Regardless of the day, or time, you will see all types of active people, and their dogs, enjoying the outdoors. You almost forget that you are in the city.

The Ross Barnett Reservoir is also located in the city of Ridgeland. During the months of March through October, you will see boats, kayaks and fisherman on and along the banks. If you are looking to rent one while visiting, I would recommend contacting Pearl River Kayaks or the Main Harbor Store and inquire about rates and availability. It is important to know that wild alligators do live in the Reservoir and the connecting tributaries, you can still enjoy a day on the water, just be vigilant.

If spending time on the water, and near 'gators,' isn't your thing there are many dining options located on the reservoir where sit you near the water and enjoy the breeze and views. A few of the local hotspots include: Pelican Cove and Shaggy's.

> *"I live by the sea, but the body of water I have the most feeling about is the Mississippi River, where I used to row and skate, ride on the ferry, watch the logs or just dream."*

–Susan Glaspell

29. CENTRAL MS– VICKSBURG, MS

If you are staying in the Central Mississippi Region and looking for a quick day trip you can follow Interstate 20 West from Jackson and be in Vicksburg in under an hour's drive. This city is most commonly known for the political and social unrest during the Civil War Era and the role it played in the outcome of the War. Driving throughout the city you will see mementos in remembrance to those who played a role during the Civil War:

- City street names
- Busts of Generals and soldiers that fought
- The Vicksburg National Military Park

If you are looking for something unrelated to this era, I would recommend heading downtown to Washington Street. Surrounded by locally owned shops, restaurants, and businesses sits the Biedenharn Coca-Cola Museum. Unbeknownst to many, the original bottlers of Coca-Cola were located within Vicksburg and began in 1894.

Vicksburg has many things to do when visiting the city; rooftop restaurants, casinos, and homes dating back to the 1700's that you can tour. The most important thing that I would recommend when visiting this city is to bring comfortable shoes and a camera to capture your memories.

"The gifts of God should be enjoyed by all citizens in Mississippi."

–Medgar Evers

30. THE PINE BELT

While traveling through this region of Mississippi, you will notice the abundance of tall, Longleaf Pine Trees that line the roadways through the southeast region of the state.

31. THE PINES- CITIES TO VISIT

The "Piney Woods" is another name for The Pine Belt in Mississippi, this region is bounded between the I-20 and I-10 Interstates. The best cities to spend time in this region include:

- Brookhaven- Driving through the main square of this quaint, picturesque town you will quickly notice that streets are lined with businesses owned by local families.
- Hattiesburg- This city is home to not one, but two colleges: The University of

Southern Mississippi and William Carey University.

- McComb- Founded and formed due to the railroad in 1872, McComb boasts a colorful history including strikes, riots, and the Civil Rights Movement.
- Natchez- Sitting on the banks of the Mississippi River, this city was known as a center for cotton planters and trading routes along the Mississippi.

"You gotta understand- the state of Mississippi was in rebellion. It had rebelled against the United States. Now that has been a very difficult story for America to tell, but that's what actually happened."

– James Meredith

32. THE PINES- BROOKHAVEN, MS

Nestled at the beginning of The Pine Belt, upon entering this town you will notice that it stands out immediately because of its southern charm. In 1856, the city was founded through the connection that the railroad brought. The railroad created access to Memphis, Tennessee and New Orleans, Louisiana. The importance of the railroad is still visible today, the town square surrounds the train station located in the middle of Downtown Brookhaven.

When visiting Brookhaven, a favorite pastime is visiting the local businesses and shopping. The town boasts over 30 boutique storefronts, all of which are locally owned. There are also over 20 locally owned restaurants, many of which use regionally sourced ingredients and have menus that will give you taste of true southern cuisine.

Every year and through each season, Brookhaven has an abundance of events that the city puts on. Depending on the time of your visit, I would highly recommend looking to see what is on the events calendar for the town. A glimpse into Brookhaven events that visitors attend:

- Annual Brookstock Festival
- Fall and Summer Fairs
- Summer Concert Series
- Wildlife and Outdoor Expo

Brookhaven is a town that has embraced an entrepreneurial spirit. It is evident in the abundance of family-owned businesses, some that have been there for generations. To fully experience what Brookhaven has to offer have you need to go off the main strip and away from the national chain names, you won't be disappointed in this decision.

Some personal favorites that should be added to your itinerary: breakfast from Janie's Pastry Shop, lunch at Pappas Pizza Pi and dinner at Georgia Blue. Catch a show at the Brookhaven Little Theatre in the evening and don't forget to book a room at the Inn on Whitworth (voted online as the best hotel in Mississippi).

"The funny response to 'One Mississippi' continues to be that people don't know what is true and what is fiction."

– Tig Notaro

33. THE PINES– HATTIESBURG, MS

Home of the Golden Eagles, The University of Southern Mississippi is a big draw for many visitors to Hattiesburg. Cloaked in black and gold, the university is a part of Conference USA for athletic competitions. If you are visiting during the fall, grab some colored apparel and take a visit to "The Rock," also known as MM Roberts Stadium to watch a game. The football season runs September through November, with most games falling on a Saturday. There are many other collegiate sporting events that can be attended on the Southern Miss Campus including: basketball, soccer, volleyball, and many more.

Other than Southern Mississippi's campus and sporting events, Hattiesburg is a city deeply rooted in its history. The Civil Rights Movement, "the Blues," and the U.S. military have all played a significant role in the development of Hattiesburg. Popular museums include: The African American History Museum, Freedom Summer Trail, and the Mississippi Armed Forces Museum.

Whether you are looking for local dining, coffee shops or a spot to grab drinks in the evening, the assortment of options in town is endless. For lunch or dinner, stop into T-Bones Records and Café. Functioning as a bookstore and coffee shop, you can browse the vinyl collection while grabbing a bite to eat. In the evening, there are many great options for where grab a drink, I would recommend visiting the Southern Prohibition Brewery in town. The taproom is open Wednesday through Saturday, but take a look at their events calendar for any upcoming celebrations during your visit.

> *"Baseball is the President tossing out the first ball of the season. And a scrubby schoolboy playing catch with his dad on a Mississippi farm."*

> – Ernie Harwell

34. THE PINES- MCCOMB, MS

Similar to many other cities across the state of Mississippi, McComb was founded due to the extension of the railroad. In 1872 McComb was founded as a new location for the maintenance shop for the railway that ran from New Orleans to Jackson. Once the maintenance shop was established, it didn't take long for shops and businesses to begin growing in what is now Downtown McComb.

There are many activities, both inside and outside to experience during your visit. The McComb City Railroad Depot Museum is "one of the South's best-preserved railroad history collections." In fact, many train enthusiasts call the museum one of the best rail museums south of Chicago. With more than 1,000 historical artifacts, the museum also has a life-sized, restored steam locomotive for you to view. Open Monday through Saturday, the museum also offers special events including "Christmas by the Tracks."

Due to its location in the Pine Belt, McComb offers many parks for you to go and explore. One park many visitors recommend is the Percy Quin State Park. There you have an opportunity to hunt, fish, canoe, hike, kayak, bike, golf, walk on the trails, and camp.

"I was just a small boy from Mississippi, and now little kids are going to identify with me through this game."

– Jerry Rice

35. THE PINES-NATCHEZ, MS

A once-prominent city during the antebellum years, Natchez was the center of the Mississippi cotton industry and vital to the trade route due to its location on the Mississippi River. While driving through the city you will be able to feel as if you are going back in time. Streets are lined with old plantation homes, all of which are *huge* in size. Due to the quantity of preserved plantation homes in the city, many are available to tour throughout the year.

Though Natchez doesn't have Windsor Castle, it does have something equally as unique; the Windsor

Ruins. Upon arrival, you will feel as though you are in Rome visiting the ancient city where buildings have collapsed and only ruins remain. When in fact, you are not in Rome, but in Natchez, Mississippi, viewing the 23, still standing, Corinthian columns that date back to 1890. The remains of the Windsor Mansion were once a part of the largest Antebellum Greek style mansion in the state of Mississippi. When visiting Natchez, I would recommend this as a place to visit. In fact, I would add it to the top of your list when visiting Mississippi.

For a scenic drive, you can hop on to the Natchez Trace. During the 19th century, the Trace was developed to allow captains and crews the ability to transfer their goods to and from the Mississippi River in Natchez. The Natchez Trace begins in Nashville, Tennessee, travels throughout the states of Tennessee and Mississippi, over nearly 440 miles and ending in Natchez, Mississippi. With its development, the Trace allowed traders to transfer goods between the Cumberland River in Tennessee and the Mississippi River. Today drivers can travel on the Trace, enjoy gorgeous views and also access the historical markers that line the original trail.

"Forty percent of the United States drains into the Mississippi. It's agriculture. It's golf courses. It's domestic runoff from our lawns and roads. Ultimately, where does it go? Downstream into the Gulf."

– Sylvia Earle

36. THE GULF COAST

Located between Louisiana and Alabama, the Mississippi Gulf Coast is 62 miles long and sitting on beautiful beaches perfect for sunbathing, fishing, or dolphin watching. Before planning your trip, be sure to look online for any events or festivals occurring during your visit!

37. THE COAST- CITIES TO VISIT

Whether you're looking to relax or play, the Gulf Coast has something for everyone. With all the cities that city on the coast, each one is a little bit different. Know what you're looking for during your trip? Here are some cities on where to find that:

- Bay St. Louis- Since the devastation of Hurricane Katrina in 2005, this city on the bay has been fighting and making a comeback drawing visitors in with its charm and appeal.
- Biloxi- Located directly on the Mississippi Sound, just past the barrier islands lies the Gulf of Mexico.
- Ocean Springs- Across the bay from Biloxi, Ocean Springs is a small, laid-back beach town offering waterfront views without the hustle and bustle of a tourist-filled city.
- Pascagoula - Once the home of the Pascagoula Native American Tribe, this town on the Pascagoula River is home to

history and the legends of the Tribe prior to the arrival of European Settlers.

"I'm from a small town on the bottom edge of Mississippi, very near New Orleans and the Louisiana border. My family has lived there for generations."

– Jesmyn Ward

38. THE COAST– BAY ST. LOUIS, MS

The backdrop for Bay St. Louis is a beautiful mixture of marshes, rivers, and beaches on the Gulf of Mexico. This charming beach town doesn't attract the same quantity of visitors that other surrounding Gulf Coast beaches might, but that just means that you have more sand and less traffic. You will be able to get the experience of a local.

When looking for the best beach, make sure to lay your towel down to the end of Main Street. You can take the walking path for three miles along the beach and find the softest sand and the prettiest view. If you're looking to fish, you can cast a line out on the pier located next to the walking bridge connecting the city to Pass Christian.

Looking for a break from the sand? Dust your feet off and head towards downtown. Here you can find the first of four unique tree trunk carvings. These creations are dubbed as the Angel Trees of Bay St. Louis. They once lived as beautiful Oak trees, now have a second life looking over the city as their watching angels. Each one has its own style and story for how they came to be beautiful living works of art.

Before leaving the city make sure to stop into The Mockingbird Café. Posed as a coffee house by day, the location transforms into a restaurant and pub in the evening. Have a four-legged friend that is a family member traveling with you? The beach is one of the few in Mississippi that is dog-friendly, you are in luck because many restaurants in town also have seating for those with a "fur-child."

"The Turkey Oak can grow practically submerged within the wetlands of Mississippi, its leaves soft as a newborn's skin."

– Hope Jahren

39. THE COAST- BILOXI, MS

The city of Biloxi has a little bit of everything for anyone who is visiting. While known as being one of the state's "hottest spots" for casinos, Biloxi has much more to offer than just that. White sandy beaches, fresh and deep sea fishing charters, top-notch golf courses, and historic museums are other activities in Biloxi.

After having fun in the sun during the day with one of these many activities, you can settle down in a chair to sit back and watch the Biloxi Shuckers. The Shuckers are a minor-league AA affiliate of the Milwaukee Brewers. If you want to put your dancing shoes on, you can also visit one of the many clubs that the casino scene also offers. I would recommend visiting the events calendar of Biloxi before your visit, many casinos will have concerts and guest DJ appearances during the summer and fall seasons. While visiting downtown you can also look up the Coast Transit Casino Hopper Shuttle which serves the casinos, attractions and businesses along the main strip, running throughout the entire week.

Of course, when visiting the Mississippi Gulf coast you will need to sample some of the local cuisines. Many of the restaurants that are serving seafood actually get their shipment from right in their backyard, no frozen fish here! Featured on The Food Network, Mary Mahoney's is located in one of the oldest homes in America and serving some delicious southern-inspired food with a Cajun twist.

"The Mississippi Coast is not like South Florida."

– Ellen Gilchrist

40. THE COAST– OCEAN SPRINGS, MS

If your idea of a perfect beach get-away is calm ocean waters, soft white sand, and little to no traffic, you need to visit Ocean Springs. This little city is, personally, my favorite beach town in the state!

Directly across the bridge from Biloxi, Ocean Springs is nestled away. When you check in for your stay at Front Beach Cottages or the Roost, rest assure that you won't be needing a car the rest of your stay. Everything that you could possibly need is within walking distance, coffee shops, restaurants, the beach; it's all right at the end of your finger-tips!

If you are looking to add some activity to your sunbathing schedule feel free to go fish on the pier with the locals and listen to their stories. You can also rent some paddleboards at Paddles Up where they will deliver and pick up the paddleboards once you are done renting for the day.

A local hotspot to grab a bite at is Government Street Grocery. Specializing in hamburgers and homemade French fries, the reviews always rave about the atmosphere and the value of the menu! If you are looking to take a short drive, I would also recommend taking a visit to The Shed Barbecue & Blues Joint.

The Shed has been featured on The Food Network and what makes this place unique is the atmosphere at this generational run family business. House specials include: baby back ribs, chicken "wangs," and brisket. Do yourself a favor and make a visit, also pack an extra shirt….just in case.

"Everyone thinks that because you're from the south you know everyone down there, but it's not like that; I never knew nothing about no Mississippi."

– Buddy Guy

41. THE COAST– PASCAGOULA, MS

Originally founded as a sleepy fishing village, the city of Pascagoula exploded after World War II with the shipbuilding industry. Since then the city has continued to grow, bounced back from Hurricane Katrina, and expanded into the oil industry with many refineries located offshore from the coast.

For an opportunity you can only find next to a body of water, visit the city's lighthouse, the Round Island Lighthouse is now located within the city. Until 1998 the Lighthouse was located on Round Island in the Mississippi Sound, after-which it was relocated. During your visit you can learn about the vast history, the impact the environment has had, and how it was reconstructed to preserve its history.

Take a trip off the mainland and visit Petit Bois Island, a part of the Gulf Islands National Seashore. The meaning of the island's name is "little woods," dating back to when the French explorers founded this sandy and sparsely covered island. While there is no entrance fee, the island is accessible by boat only. You can casily contact one of the many fishing charters to plan a trip out to the island and sit in awe of the natural beauty and take a step back from the hustle and bustle of city life.

42. FESTIVAL GETAWAYS

Perhaps you want to plan your visit during an annual festival that celebrates the heritage and culture of Mississippi. Throughout the state of Mississippi, each region holds unique festivals relative to the history and region they are located in. There are many more than what is listed below, however, these are some of my favorite, can't miss annual festivals:

- Crusin' the Coast- The Coast, Gulf Coast cities
  Nicknamed "Americans Largest Block Party," Crusin' the Coast is held every fall and travels along the Mississippi Gulf Coast. You can view vintage cars which have been preserved in prime condition, listen to great music from the 50s and 60s, and enjoy other events such as Sock Hops, and Car Corrals. This is an event not worth missing in the fall.
- Elvis Festival- The Triangle, Tupelo
  Held in honor of Tupelo's native son, Elvis, the festival is a celebration of his life and a way to honor his memory. The festival takes

place during the summer and includes a variety of different activities: a 5K marathon, parades, after parties, and of course live music! The schedule of events runs from Thursday through Sunday and it never disappoints.

- Juke Joint Festival- The Delta, Clarksdale
Dedicated to all the late Delta Blues performers that have passed away during the past year and unforgettable Delta Blues musicians, the JJF commemorates the lives they led and music they left behind. Advertised as "half Blues festival, half small-town fair and all about the Delta," the festival represents all that is great about the Mississippi Delta: music, food, and community. Traditionally the festival is held during the spring, this is an event you don't want to miss. I'll go on the record and say that you can't find a place like the Mississippi Delta anywhere else in the world.

- Mudbug Bash- The Hills, Hernando
Looking for a festival that embellishes *true* southern decadence? During the spring

make sure to visit the Mudbug Bash. Mudbugs (see tip #46) are at the center of this festival. Held outside, this festival features all-you-can-eat crawfish, with all the fixin's (lots of corn on the cob and potatoes). There is also live music and samplings from local restaurants. Embrace this southern-style festival and plan a visit, I promise you won't leave hungry.

- Natchez Food and Wine Festival- The Pines, Natchez

  To visit the "Tastings along the Mississippi River" add the Natchez Food and Wine Festival to your Mississippi Bucket List. With over 700 attendees, this event is highly anticipated every fall. The best wine and beverage brokers are in attendance, along with craft brewers who brew at home and craft brewmasters. The festival is filled with live music, laughter from the community, and scrumptious food! Get your tickets early to ensure you get the best seats and at the best prices!

- St Patrick's Day Festival- Central MS, Jackson

Each year, the weekend before or after St. Patrick's Day, the city of Jackson hosts the annual St. Patrick's Day Festival. An all-day event, the day begins with a parade in Downtown Jackson followed by an all-day party at Hal and Mal's Downtown. First started when locals dressed up and celebrating in their shamrock green, it has turned into one of the top festivals in the state. The parade is family friendly, but be sure to get your tickets early for the after party and find a sitter for the kids. P.S. Don't forget to wear your green or risk getting pinched.

43. MISSISSIPPI'S HOT TAMALE TRAIL

What is the first thing you think of when you think of Mississippi... cotton, catfish, the River? One thing that probably isn't first to mind, tamales. How, when, and why tamales are now a staple piece within the Mississippi Delta region has as many theories as there are recipes. Mississippi folklore will tell you that it was migrant Mexican workers who arrived for the cotton harvest, others will say soldiers brought the recipe back after the U.S.-Mexican War. Regardless of how they got their origin in Mississippi, The Tamale Trail, as a result, is now a must-visit within the state.

Though a staple within the Delta Region, the Hot Tamale Trail spreads across all of Mississippi. A couple of my favorite hot spots include: Solly's Hot Tamales and Fat Mama's Hot Tamales. Look online for the interactive map showing the entire Mississippi Hot Tamale Trail. On the map, you will find over 30 stop locations along the Mississippi Tamale Trail located in all regions of the state.

44. (LEGAL) CASINO SPORTS BOOKS

During the summer of 2018, the United States Supreme Court in Washington D.C. confirmed that sports betting would be legal in all 50 states, previously it was only allowed in Las Vegas, Nevada. What's that got to do with Mississippi? The state of Mississippi was one of the first states, besides Nevada, to legalize the sport.

While bringing in residual funding for the state, legal sportsbooks now offer a new way for residents and visitors to gamble. The sportsbooks are located throughout the state at different casinos, if you are feeling lucky you can head on over and place your bets, some of the sportsbooks include:

- The Beau Rivage, Biloxi, MS
- The Gold Strike Casino, Tunica, MS
- The Riverwalk Casino, Vicksburg, MS

45. FOLLOW THE BLUES TRAIL MARKERS

Established in 2007, The Mississippi Blue Trail commemorates historical sites "related to the birth, growth and influence of the Blues throughout the state of Mississippi." Located along the Gulf Coast, on the Natchez Trace, throughout the Pine Belt and Central Mississippi, up through the Delta and the Triangle, the Trail travels through all regions of the state.

More than anything the "Blues Trail is a way to tell stories through words and images of bluesmen and women and how the places where they lived and the times in which they existed- and continue to exist- influenced the music." Markers are located along state highways, within small towns, in cemeteries and even in clubs and churches. During your travels be on the lookout for these markers, each one has a different story of the Magnolia State and how it came to be. A few, of the many, Trail marker locations can be found in:

- Ackerman, MS
- Bentonia, MS
- Berclair, MS
- Clarksdale, MS
- Cleveland, MS
- Como, MS
- Forrest, MS
- Indianola, MS
- Lexington, MS
- Tunica, MS
- Yazoo City, MS

When you pass these locations, don't forget to stop and read the markers. In a mere five minutes or less, you will be able to learn a little bit more of what differentiates Mississippi from any other state in the Union.

46. HOW TO EAT THROUGH MISSISSIPPI

Influenced from the Gulf with fresh seafood, Cajun and Creole cooking from the south, barbecue from the north, and with fresh catfish from the 'Sip River, recipes and flavors in Mississippi food can vary drastically. During your visit to Mississippi, the following are a must-know before stepping foot into any restaurant or eatery:

- BBQ
  Being located on the Mississippi River, in the same fashion that goods that have been traded over the years along the routes, so have the barbecue recipes. Before ordering, always be sure to confirm what style of barbecue the restaurant is serving up, in Mississippi it can be influenced by any style: Memphis, St. Louis, and sometimes even Carolina.

- Biscuits
  These are a staple breakfast and brunch item. Just know, you cannot order gravy on the side.
- Blue Plate
  Defined as "a restaurant meal consisting of a full main course ordered as a single menu item." On many Mississippi menus, you will find 'Blue Plate Specials.' With these specials, different days of the week consist of different specialties that are available to order. Typically you will get a meat, with two or three sides, a dessert and a drink all included in one price. While both fulfilling and economically conscious, you will have a food baby once you're done eating. A word of advice, get the dessert to-go, you can thank me later.
- Catfish and Hush Puppies
  Catfish, cotton, and Mississippi are synonymous with one another. When you order catfish, know it was probably farm-raised in the state (see tip #14). As chips are to fish in England, hushpuppies are to catfish. A traditional item, crispy balls of

seasoned cornbread, they are served next to the catfish fillet or strips that you order.

- Comeback Sauce
  A cross between Thousand Island dressing and remoulade (famous in New Orleans), this creamy dip has a little bit of a kick. Take a look at on the menu at any restaurant you visit in Mississippi and it is probably on there. It can be in the form of a dressing, dipping sauce or spread, you're bound to see it on every menu across the state. Order it on the side and give it a shot!

- Fried Chicken
  While the state bird is the Mockingbird, it might as well be the chicken. Served everywhere from roadside gas stations, brunch (Chicken and Waffles anyone?), to fine dining locations you will find some type of fried chicken on the menu. Pair it with a glass of Sweet Tea and you've got yourself a meal sent down from the heavens.

- Hot Tamales
  See tip #43 for the history on the Mississippi Hot Tamale Trail. FYI, you can never go

wrong ordering this on any menu during
your visit to the state.

- Mudbugs (aka crawfish)
Crawfish boils are a staple to Mississippi
cuisine during the spring every year. A feast
celebrated with good friends and good food,
crawfish boils can be held in backyards, at
festivals, and at parties. Simple to coordinate
and quick to cook, your plate will be full of
mudbugs, corn-on-the-cob and potatoes. Just
be aware of the spice if you aren't used to it,
otherwise your face will turn red and you
may be begging for water or another beer.
*This was my dad's first experience with a
true, *southern,* all-you-can-eat crawfish boil
in the 'Sip years ago.

- Soul Food
Soul food can also be referred to as 'country
cookin'." Many recipes are staple pieces
(think grits, okra, and greens) and have been
passed down for generations. Don't worry,
you won't be disappointed eating any
variety, you just may need a nap after eating
them.

47. HOW TO DRINK THROUGH MISSISSIPPI

During recent years a number of local distilleries and breweries have begun popping up in Mississippi across all regions. Many offer tours and tastings available during different days of the week:

- Biloxi Brewing Company- Biloxi, MS
- Chandeleur Island Brewing Company- Gulfport, MS
- Crooked Letter Brewery- Ocean Springs, MS
- Key City Brewing Company- Vicksburg, MS
- Lazy Magnolia Brewing Company- Kiln, MS
- Lucky Town Brewing Company- Jackson, MS
- Mayhew Junction Brewing Company- Greenville, MS
- Mississippi Brewing Company- Gulfport, MS
- Natchez Brewing Company- Natchez, MS

- Slowboat Brewing Company- Laurel, MS
- Southern Prohibition Brewing Company- Hattiesburg, MS
- Threefoot Brewing Company- Meridian, MS
- Yalobusha Brewing Company- Water Valley, MS
- 1817 Brewery- Okolona, MS

The Mississippi Distillery Trail also includes an abundance of local distilleries located all over the state. Tours can include craft distillery and farm tours that will educate and also entertain visitors. Be sure to visit the many located all over the state:

- Cathead Distillery- Jackson (Central MS)
- Charboneau Distillery- Natchez (The Pines)
- Rich Distilling- Canton (Central MS)

48. HONORABLE MENTIONS

Although many attractions located throughout the state have been mentioned in these 50 tips, unfortunately not all could be mentioned. In order to provide you with the most information for your visit, in this tip you will find all 'honorable mentions' and other must-visit locations for your trip to Mississippi:

- All American Rose Garden- Located on the campus of the University of Southern Mississippi, you can take a walk through the public garden.
- Biloxi Lighthouse- With the backdrop of the Gulf behind it, the Biloxi Lighthouse is the perfect place for a photo opportunity.
- Blessing of the Fleet Festival- During this festival, the food and music are flowing, enjoy some Gulf Coast seafood while attending the almost, century-old, annual tradition.
- Brent's Drugs- A staple to Jackson, you can feel as if you are taking a trip back in time to the 1960s, also a location where *The Help* was filmed.
- Cypress Swamp- Located on the Natchez Trace you can experience visiting a swamp, while still being near the Jackson city limits.
- Eudora Welty House and Garden- Take a tour to the home of the Pulitzer Prize-

winning author that was born in the Magnolia State.

- Grammy Museum- An interactive museum, you can learn about the musical achievements of Mississippians.
- Mammy's Cupboard- Stop in for lunch while traveling on Mississippi State Highway 61, everything is homemade from scratch and will make your mouth water.
- Mississippi State Fair- Held annually during the fall, you can indulge in some fried food as well as other homemade specialty items.
- Shack Up Inn- Do you believe in trading your soul for the Blues? Here Robert Johnson traded his soul, or so the story goes...
- Tishomingo State Park- Take a trip back in time while walking over the swinging bridge. The state park holds the American history prior to the European settlement in the area.

49. DON'T FORGET TO PACK

The weather in Mississippi can be humid, the bugs plentiful and there is always a possibility of a pop-up rain shower. Before visiting, here are a few things you will need to pack in your bag or pick up along the way:

- Allergy medication – Mississippi is one of the worst states in the country for people with allergies, don't let that stop you though just come prepared.

- Bug Spray- Although bugs can be seasonal, it would be a good idea to bring bug spray to fight off the mosquitos that are in abundance during the spring, summer and early fall.

- Deodorant- You're in the Deep South, you're probably going to sweat.

- Extra Pair of Socks- *See note above.

- Sunglasses- Protect your eyes from the high-rising Mississippi sun.

- Sunscreen- Also protect your skin from the Mississippi sun.

- Tennis Shoes- Bring an extra pair just in case you want to walk along some historic trails.

- Flip Flop Sandals- Even if you're not visiting the Coast, fresh bodies of water are located all over the state.

If you have these packed in your bag, you should be ready to go in any situation you encounter during your visit to Mississippi.

50. MANNERS MATTER

Perhaps the most important piece of information, in addition to tip #3, would be this final tip; manners matter. During your visit to Mississippi, keep in mind that you are visiting a southern state; a region of United States that is known for decadence and cotillions. Manners matter because they remind us of 'the good ole days," and in Mississippi we always want to leave our best impression on someone before we leave them. A few things you should remember during your visit:

- Arrive on Time- For reservations, events and tours, always arrive on time.

- Attire- Whether you are going to a fancy dinner or to the store, make sure you are put-together and looking appropriate. "Sunday's Best" dress doesn't apply at all times in the South, but many Southerners take pride in their appearance in public. Enjoy it and dress up a little, never feel overdressed, remember you're in the South, someone will always be more over-dressed than you.

- Bourbon- Never order this with Coke. Order on the rocks (over ice), neat, or with water.

Also a good note: only the good bourbon comes from Kentucky (think Eagle Rare, Maker's Mark or Woodford)

- Chivalry- Gentlemen, this one is for you. Hold the doors open, pull out seats at the table and let her order first. These will go a long way with any interaction with a lady.

- Common Courtesy- Say hello, or give a simple head nod or smile during every interaction…even when passing strangers. A "good morning, how are you?" will go a long way.

- Greetings- A first impression can only be made once; have a firm handshake, make eye contact, and smile.

- Mind Your Ps & Ts- Never forget to say "please" and "thank you."

- Technology- Put your cell phones away when sitting at the dinner table, focus on spending time with one another.

Keep these simple tips in mind during your visit and you'll leave as an honorary Mississippian.

TOP REASONS TO BOOK THIS TRIP

Music: The "Birthplace of American Music" is a title Mississippi is proud of, anywhere in the state that you will visit you will experience this first-hand.

Food: With specialties including seafood, tamales and southern cooking, you can bet the entrees, flavor and seasonings will make your taste buds water.

The Soul: No matter where you are in Mississippi you will feel the soul in the music and see the soul in the people and food.

READ OTHER
GREATER THAN A TOURIST
BOOKS

Greater Than a Tourist San Miguel de Allende Guanajuato Mexico:
50 Travel Tips from a Local by Tom Peterson

Greater Than a Tourist – Lake George Area New York USA:
50 Travel Tips from a Local by Janine Hirschklau

Greater Than a Tourist – Monterey California United States:
50 Travel Tips from a Local by Katie Begley

Greater Than a Tourist – Chanai Crete Greece:
50 Travel Tips from a Local by Dimitra Papagrigoraki

Greater Than a Tourist – The Garden Route Western Cape Province
South Africa: 50 Travel Tips from a Local by Li-Anne McGregor van
Aardt

Greater Than a Tourist – Sevilla Andalusia Spain:
50 Travel Tips from a Local by Gabi Gazon

Greater Than a Tourist – Kota Bharu Kelantan Malaysia:
50 Travel Tips from a Local by Aditi Shukla

Children's Book: Charlie the Cavalier Travels the World by Lisa
Rusczyk

> TOURIST

Visit Greater Than a Tourist for Free Travel Tips
http://GreaterThanATourist.com

Sign up for the Greater Than a Tourist Newsletter for
discount days, new books, and travel information:
http://eepurl.com/cxspyf

Follow us on Facebook for tips, images, and ideas:
https://www.facebook.com/GreaterThanATourist

Follow us on Pinterest for travel tips and ideas:
http://pinterest.com/GreaterThanATourist

Follow us on Instagram for beautiful travel images:
http://Instagram.com/GreaterThanATourist

> TOURIST

Please leave your honest review of this book on Amazon and Goodreads. Please send your feedback to GreaterThanaTourist@gmail.com as we continue to improve the series. We appreciate your positive and constructive feedback. Thank you.

METRIC CONVERSIONS

TEMPERATURE

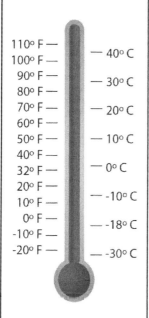

110° F —   — 40° C
100° F —
90° F —   — 30° C
80° F —
70° F —   — 20° C
60° F —
50° F —   — 10° C
40° F —
32° F —   — 0° C
20° F —
10° F —   — -10° C
0° F —   — -18° C
-10° F —
-20° F —   — -30° C

To convert F to C:

Subtract 32, and then multiply by 5/9 or .5555.

To Convert C to F:

Multiply by 1.8
and then add 32.

32F = 0C

LIQUID VOLUME

To Convert:.................Multiply by
U.S. Gallons to Liters................ 3.8
U.S. Liters to Gallons 26
Imperial Gallons to U.S. Gallons 1.2
Imperial Gallons to Liters....... 4.55
Liters to Imperial Gallons 22
1 Liter = .26 U.S. Gallon
1 U.S. Gallon = 3.8 Liters

DISTANCE

To convert ....Multiply by
Inches to Centimeters 2.54
Centimeters to Inches 39
Feet to Meters...................... .3
Meters to Feet 3.28
Yards to Meters 91
Meters to Yards 1.09
Miles to Kilometers 1.61
Kilometers to Miles............ .62
1 Mile = 1.6 km
1 km = .62 Miles

WEIGHT

1 Ounce = .28 Grams
1 Pound = .4555 Kilograms
1 Gram = .04 Ounce
1 Kilogram = 2.2 Pounds

TRAVEL QUESTIONS

- Do you bring presents home to family or friends after a vacation?

- Do you get motion sick?

- Do you have a favorite billboard?

- Do you know what to do if there is a flat tire?

- Do you like a sun roof open?

- Do you like to eat in the car?

- Do you like to wear sun glasses in the car?

- Do you like toppings on your ice cream?

- Do you use public bathrooms?

- Did you bring your cell phone and does it have power?

- Do you have a form of identification with you?

- Have you ever been pulled over by a cop?

- Have you ever given money to a stranger on a road trip?

- Have you ever taken a road trip with animals?

- Have you ever went on a vacation alone?

- Have you ever run out of gas?

- If you could move to any place in the world, where would it be?

- If you could travel anywhere in the world, where would you travel?

- If you could travel in any vehicle, which one would it be?

- If you had three things to wish for from a magic genie, what would they be?

- If you have a driver's license, how many times did it take you to pass the test?

- What are you the most afraid of on vacation?

- What do you want to get away from the most when you are on vacation?

- What foods smells bad to you?

- What item do you bring on ever trip with you away from home?

- What makes you sleepy?

- What song would you love to hear on the radio when you're cruising on the highway?

- What travel job would you want the least?

- What will you miss most while you are away from home?

- What is something you always wanted to try?

- What is the best road side attraction that you ever saw?

- What is the farthest distance you ever biked?

- What is the farthest distance you ever walked?

- What is the weirdest thing you needed to buy while on vacation?

- What is your favorite candy?

- What is your favorite color car?

- What is your favorite family vacation?

- What is your favorite food?

- What is your favorite gas station drink or food?

- What is your favorite license plate design?

- What is your favorite restaurant?

- What is your favorite smell?

- What is your favorite song?

- What is your favorite sound that nature makes?

- What is your favorite thing to bring home from a vacation?

- What is your favorite vacation with friends?

- What is your favorite way to relax?

- Where is the farthest place you ever traveled in a car?

- Where is the farthest place you ever went North, South, East and West?

- Where is your favorite place in the world?

- Who is your favorite singer?

- Who taught you how to drive?

- Who will you miss the most while you are away?

- Who if the first person you will contact when you get to your destination?

- Who brought you on your first vacation?

- Who likes to travel the most in your life?

- Would you rather be hot or cold?

- Would you rather drive above, below, or at the speed limited?

- Would you rather drive on a highway or a back road?

- Would you rather go on a train or a boat?

- Would you rather go to the beach or the woods?

TRAVEL BUCKET LIST

1.

2.

3.

4.

5.

6.

7.

8.

9.

10.

NOTES

Made in the USA
Columbia, SC
03 July 2021

41363909R00074